KT-510-440

Little Miss Shy

Little Miss Fickle

Little Miss Naughty

Little Miss Busy-Body

Little Miss Lucky

Little Miss Trouble

Little Miss Chatterbox

Little Miss Splendid

Little Miss Scatterbrain

MR.MEN **LITTLE MISS**

This edition © Robert Frederick Ltd. 1997
Old Orchard Street, Bath BA1 1JU

Printed in Singapore by Welpac Printing & Packaging Pte Ltd.

Little Miss

BIRTHDAY BOOK

Birth Signs

(March 21-April 20) **ARIES**

Fiery First Sign
Symbol: The Ram
Ruling Planet: Mars
Birthstone: Diamond
Flower: Sweet Pea
Colours: Fiery Red, Orange
Numbers: Seven, Six
Day: Tuesday

TAURUS *(April 21-May 21)*

Earthy Second Sign
Symbol: The Bull
Ruling Planet: Venus
Birthstone: Emerald
Flower: Lily of the Valley
Colours: Natural colour
Numbers: One, Nine
Day: Friday

(May 22-June 21) **GEMINI**

Airy Third Sign
Symbol: The Twins
Ruling Planet: Mercury
Birthstone: Agate
Flower: Rose
Colours: Sky Blue, Black
Numbers: Three, Four
Day: Wednesday

CANCER *(June 22-July 22)*

Watery Fourth Sign
Symbol: Crab, Moon
Ruling Planet: The Moon
Birthstone: Moonstone, Pearl
Flower: Larkspur
Colours: Silver, Sea Green
Numbers: Eight, Three
Day: Friday

Birth Signs

(July 23-August 23) LEO

Fiery & Fixed Fifth Sign
Symbol: The Sun, The Lion
Ruling Planet: The Sun
Birthstone: Sardonyx
Flower: Gladioli
Colours: Gold, Fiery Shades
Numbers: Five, Nine
Day: Sunday

VIRGO (August 24-Sept 22)

Earthy & Adaptable Sixth Sign
Symbol: Fertility Goddess
Ruling Planet: Mercury
Birthstone: Sapphire
Flower: Aster
Colours: Natural, Warm
Numbers: Eight, Four
Day: Wednesday

(Sept 23-Oct 23) LIBRA

Airy Sociable Seventh Sign
Symbol: The Scales
Ruling Planet: Venus
Birthstone: Opal
Flower: Calendula
Colours: Peacock Blue
Numbers: Six, Nine
Day: Friday

SCORPIO (Oct 24-Nov 22)

Watery Eighth Sign
Symbol: The Scorpion
Ruling Planet: Mars
Birthstone: Topaz
Flower: Chrysanthemum
Colours: Dark Water Shades
Numbers: Three, Five
Day: Tuesday

Birth Signs

(Nov 23-Dec 23) SAGITTARIUS

Fiery, Adaptable Ninth Sign
Symbol: The Archer
Ruling Planet: Jupiter
Birthstone: Turquoise
Flower: Narcissus
Colours: Fiery Reds
Number: Nine
Day: Thursday

CAPRICORN (Dec 24-Jan 20)

Earthy Tenth Sign
Symbol: The Goat
Ruling Planet: Saturn
Birthstone: Garnet
Flower: Carnation
Colours: Restrained to Dark
Numbers: Seven, Three
Day: Saturday

(Jan 21-Feb 18) AQUARIUS

Airy, Stubborn Eleventh Sign
Symbol: Water Carrier
Ruling Planet: Uranus
Birthstone: Amethyst
Flower: Violet
Colours: Wild, Way Out
Numbers: Eight, Four
Day: Wednesday

PISCES (Feb 19-March 20)

Watery & Compromising Twelfth
Symbol: Two Fish
Ruling Planet: Neptune
Birthstone: Bloodstone
Flower: Jonquil
Colours: Violet, Oceanic
Numbers: Five, Eight
Day: Friday

January 1

January 2

January 3

January 4

January

January 5

January 6

January 7

January 8

Little Miss Bossy

. . . she is
always ordering
everyone about

January

January 9

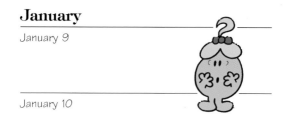

January 10

January 11

January 12

January

January 13

January 14

January 15

January 16

January

January 17

January 18

January 19

January 20

January

January 21

January 22

January 23

January 24

Little Miss Busy

. . . a workaholic who hates
to be idle, however pointless
the task

January

January 25

January 26

January 27

January 28

January

January 29

January 30

January 31

February

February 1

February 2

February 3

February 4

February

February 5

February 6

February 7

February 8

February 9

February 10

February 11

February 12

February

February 13

February 14

February 15

February 16

Little Miss Chatterbox

. . . once she starts
she can't stop talking!

February

February 17

February 18

February 19

February 20

February

February 21

February 22

February 23

February 24

February

February 25

February 26

February 27

February 28

Little Miss Contrary

. . . always does
the opposite
of what you
would expect

March

March 1

March 2

March 3

March 4

March

March 5

March 6

March 7

March 8

March 9

March 10

March 11

March 12

March

March 13

March 14

March 15

March 16

March

March 17

March 18

March 19

March 20

March

March 21

March 22

March 23

March 24

Little Miss Curious

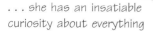

. . . she has an insatiable
curiosity about everything

March

March 25

March 26

March 27

March 28

March

March 29

March 30

March 31

April

April 1

April 2

April 3

April 4

April

April 5

April 6

April 7

April 8

Little Miss Fun

. . . she thinks
that life should be
one long party!

April 9

April 10

April 11

April 12

April

April 13

April 14

April 15

April 16

April 17

April 18

April 19

April 20

April

April 21

April 22

April 23

April 24

April 25

April 26

April 27

April 28

April

April 29

April 30

Little Miss Giggles

. . . it doesn't
matter what she is
doing she can't help but giggle

May

May 1

May 2

May 3

May 4

May

May 5

May 6

May 7

May 8

May

May 9

May 10

May 11

May 12

May

May 13

May 14

May 15

May 16

Little Miss Lucky

. . . lives in
Horseshoe Cottage,
and gets out of the worst situations by luck

May

May 17

May 18

May 19

May 20

May

May 21

May 22

May 23

May 24

May 25

May 26

May 27

May 28

May

May 29

May 30

May 31

June

June 1

June 2

June 3

June 4

June

June 5

June 6

June 7

June 8

Little Miss Naughty

. . . a mischievous imp
who usually ends up
getting a taste of her own medicine

June

June 9

___

June 10

___

June 11

___

June 12

June

June 13

June 14

June 15

June 16

June

June 17

June 18

June 19

June 20

June

June 21

June 22

June 23

June 24

Little Miss Neat

. . . she likes everything
to be spotlessly clean
and in its place

June 25

June 26

June 27

June 28

June

June 29

June 30

July 1

July 2

July 3

July 4

July

July 5

July 6

July 7

July 8

July

July 9

July 10

July 11

July 12

July

July 13

July 14

July 15

July 16

Little Miss Quick

. . . she is always in a rush and hence never completes anything properly

July

July 17

July 18

July 19

July 20

July 21

July 22

July 23

July 24

July

July 25

July 26

July 27

July 28

July 29

July 30

July 31

Little Miss Scatterbrain

. . . she is forever getting things mixed up

August

August 1

August 2

August 3

August 4

August

August 5

August 6

August 7

August 8

August

August 9

August 10

August 11

August 12

August

August 13

August 14

August 15

August 16

August 17

August 18

August 19

August 20

August

August 21

August 22

August 23

August 24

Little Miss Shy

. . . a desperately
timid character
who is constantly
blushing

August

August 25

August 26

August 27

August 28

August

August 29

August 30

August 31

September

September 1

September 2

September 3

September 4

September 5

September 6

September 7

September 8

Little Miss Somersault

. . . she is very agile and
acrobatic (and a bit of a show-off!)

September

September 9

September 10

September 11

September 12

September

September 13

September 14

September 15

September 16

September

September 17

September 18

September 19

September 20

September

September 21

September 22

September 23

September 24

September

September 25

September 26

September 27

September 28

September

September 29

September 30

Little Miss Splendid

. . . a vain and conceited character with a weakness for shopping

October

October 1

October 2

October 3

October 4

October

October 5

October 6

October 7

October 8

October

October 9

October 10

October 11

October 12

October

October 13

October 14

October 15

October 16

Little Miss Stubborn

. . . she won't change her mind once it is made up

October 17

October 18

October 19

October 20

October

October 21

October 22

October 23

October 24

October

October 25

October 26

October 27

October 28

October

October 29

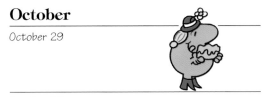

October 30

October 31

November

November 1

November 2

November 3

November 4

November

November 5

November 6

November 7

November 8

Little Miss Sunshine

. . . always cheerful
and bright, she tries
to cheer up everyone
around her

November

November 9

November 10

November 11

November 12

November

November 13

November 14

November 15

November 16

November

November 17

November 18

November 19

November 20

November

November 21

November 22

November 23

November 24

Little Miss Tiny

. . . she lives in a
mousehole in the dining
room of Home Farm

November

November 25

November 26

November 27

November 28

November

November 29

November 30

December

December 1

December 2

December 3

December 4

December

December 5

December 6

December 7

December 8

December

December 9

December 10

December 11

December 12

December

December 13

December 14

December 15

December 16

Little Miss Trouble

. . . she likes to make
mischief wherever she goes

December

December 17

December 18

December 19

December 20

December

December 21

December 22

December 23

December 24

December

December 25

December 26

December 27

December 28

December

December 29

December 30

December 31

Little Miss Twins

. . . identical twins who live in Twoland where
everything comes in twos

Notes

Little Miss Tidy

Little Miss Quick

Little Miss Magic

Little Miss Star

Little Miss Contrary

Little Miss Dotty

Little Miss Tiny

Little Miss Twins

Little Miss Naughty